eNaira
Speed Wallet

The Good, The Bad & The Ugly

By

Ojula Technology Innovations

eNaira Speed Wallet: The Good, The Bad & The Ugly

ISBN: 9798755137522

Copyright © Ojula Technology Innovations

All rights reserved

Published in the United States

Limit of Liability/Disclaimer of Warranty

This book contains information obtained from authentic and highly regarded sources. Reasonable efforts have been made to publish reliable data and information, but the author and publisher cannot assume responsibility for the validity of all materials or the consequences of their use. All information given in this book is based on the author's own research and does not constitute technical, financial or professional advice. The author and publisher have attempted to trace the copyright holders of all material reproduced in this publication, and apologize to copyright holders if permission to publish in this form has not been obtained. If any copyright material has not been acknowledged please write and let us know so we may rectify in any future reprint.

Except as permitted under U.S. Copyright Law, no part of this book may be reprinted, reproduced, transmitted, or utilized in any form by any electronic, mechanical, or other means, now known or hereafter invented, including photocopying, microfilming, and recording, or in any information storage or retrieval system, without written permission from the publisher.

Table of Contents

1. What's eNaira? 5

    1.1. Objectives & Benefits 6

    1.2. How eNaira Works...7

    1.3. What are the Impacts of eNaira on Nigeria Economy? 7

    1.4. The Dark Sides of eNaira 9

2. What is the eNaira Speed Wallet? 13

    2.1. Registration Requirements, Transaction Limits & Balances 13

    2.3. Five Types of eNaira Wallets 14

        2.3.1. eNaira Stock Wallet 14

        2.3.2. eNaira Treasury Wallet 14

        2.3.3. eNaira Branch Wallet..14

        2.3.4. eNaira Speed Merchant Wallet 14

        2.3.5. eNaira Speed Wallet 14

    2.4. eNaira Speed Wallet versus eNaira Speed Merchant Wallet ...15

    2.5. How to Download & Setup eNaira Speed Wallet 15

    2.6. How to Download & Setup eNaira Speed Merchant Wallet 33

3. The Good, The Bad & The Ugly 63

    3.1 My Evaluation..63

        3.3.1 The Good Sides of eNaira Wallets 63

        3.3.2 The Bad Sides of eNaira Wallets 64

3.3.3 The Ugly Sides of eNaira Wallets 68

3.3.4. People Experiencing Trouble with the eNaira Wallets & Why CBN is Unable to Find a Fix..69

3.2. Conclusion 70

1. What's eNaira?

Developed by Bitt (www.bitt.com), the fintech company based in the Caribbeans, eNaira is a digital currency issued by the Central Bank of Nigeria (CBN) as a new legal tender. Officially launched in October 25, 2021, eNaira is the digital form of the physical Naira that you can use the same way as physical cash. Since it's Africa's first **C**entral **B**ank **D**igital **C**urrency, eNaira is officially known by the acronym **CBDC**.

The CBN governor, Godwin Emefiele announced on October 26, 2021 that **eNaira would be free for 90 days**. In addition, the apex bank has minted 500-million-naira worth of the digital money (eNaira), and has added 33 banks so far to the eNaira platform. Here's the link to a video where Bitt CEO explains all he did in the eNaira project: https://www.youtube.com/watch?v=qRNt4L0huD4.

Primary Role of the CBN with Respect to eNaira

According to Section 2 of the CBN Act of 2007, the CBN is the issuing authority of all forms of Naira. This apex bank will also be responsible for determining the regulatory, technical, and operational standards for eNaira.

Difference between eNaira and the Naira in your Bank account

In addition to being a digital currency, eNaira is also a direct liability on the Central Bank of Nigeria whereas the Naira in your bank account is held as deposit liability by financial institutions. It's peer to peer exchanged, that is, its value is the same as fiat Naira (1 eNaira = 1 Naira). In other words, eNaira has the same value as the physical naira, therefore the exchange rate is 1 to 1.

1.1. Objectives & Benefits

According to CBN, the Apex monetary authority in Nigeria, eNaira is a fast, secure, affordable, and reliable payment option. It's designed to support the digital economy, and aid financial inclusion in Nigeria. eNaira will, among other benefits, enhance the Nigerian payment ecosystem, increase revenue and tax collection, aid targeted social interventions, and improve diaspora remittances. That's because users of eNaira can make contactless payments by simply scanning a QR code.

Benefits of eNaira

- The international community will have a little more respect for Nigeria's currency, and this may help the naira appreciate a little bit.

- The future of everything in the world is digital. Therefore, it's better Nigeria gets on board very fast. The earlier Nigerians face this new reality, the better.

- It can be used for instant settlements

- It has 99.9% reliability and service availability

- Its charges are very low

- It has no dispensing errors

- It has no reconciliation issues

- Advanced data safety, security and privacy

- If the eNaira becomes more successful, CBN will spend less money printing fiat naira. This will help reduce CBN's budget.

1.2. How eNaira Works

According to the Apex bank, eNaira will not replace cash. Instead, it will circulate alongside cash as a safe, more efficient, and cost-saving payment option. In addition, eNaira is secured with cryptographic techniques against cloning, counterfeiting, and other forms of cyber attack. Also, according to CBN, you need your accurate **BVN Data** for a hitch-free eNaira speed wallet enrolment.

To access eNaira, first you must be a bank customer. You can access eNaira by downloading one of the following apps: the eNaira Speed Wallet (for individual customers) or by downloading the eNaira Speed Merchant Wallet (for businesses or corporate organizations) in app stores such as Google Play store or Apple store. Alternatively, you can scan the QR code on the cBN's eNaira website: https://www.enaira.gov.ng/news. Use the following short codes to download the appropriate wallet from the Google Play Store.

- https://bit.ly/3pElvlY (eNaira Speed Wallet)
- https://bit.ly/2XMeGuF (eNaira Speed Merchant Wallet)

For iOS users, just search the Apple store for *eNaira Speed Wallet* or *eNaira Speed Merchant Wallet*.

1.3. What are the Impacts of eNaira on Nigeria Economy?

The eNaira or CBDC is now live after it was official launched at the State House in Abuja by the Nigeria's President, Retired General **Muhammadu Buhari** on Monday, October 25, 2021.

Fig. 1.3.1: eNaira's Launch at Abuja

This is because the earlier plan to unveil the eNaira on October 1, 2021 was shelved. According to President Muhammadu Buhari in a televised speech in Abuja, the Federal Capital,

"The adoption of the central bank digital currency and its underlying technology, called blockchain, can increase Nigeria's gross domestic product by $29 billion over the next 10 years."

Now, according to CBN, the following are the foreseen impacts of the eNaira on Nigerian Economy:

Economic Growth

Since it offers easier access to capital and financial services, eNaira is expected to increase economic activities at very low interest transaction rate.

Diaspora Remittance

eNaira makes it easier for people living in diaspora to send money to Nigeria more securely, speedily, and cheaply.

Fraud Monitoring

Since eNaira is traceable, it can be used to limit fraudulent or illicit transactions.

Social Welfare

eNaira can assist in faster, equitable and more effective distribution of cash to communities and households that are included in the government's social welfare programs.

Financial Inclusion

eNaira financial services are made available to people and communities that do not have sufficient banking opportunities.

Local and Cross-Border Trade

Since eNaira makes transactions quick, safe and cheap, it increases local and international trade.

Security

Since it cannot be forged or counterfeited, and as a result of its security structure and uniqueness, eNaira has a stronger security than the fiat Naira.

Revenue Collection

eNaira aids government in revenue collection because it reduces cash handling costs.

1.4. The Dark Sides of eNaira

First, eNaira is not a cryptocurrency, even though it uses the same underline technology. Unlike other cryptocurrencies like Bitcoin that are not backed by any established authority, eNaira is pegged against the fiat Naira and will not fluctuate due to market influence at a rate different from the fiat Naira.

No matter how much security eNaira promises, the fears of risk of this new digital currency greeted Nigerians at the launch. Even though, Godwin Emefiele the CBN Governor, has dismissed worries on eNaira's safety, many Nigerians are still expressing fears on various social media platforms.

Note that cryptocurrencies like Bitcoin had overshadowed the future of digital money as a legal tender before Nigeria's official banking channels suddenly stopped its use in February 2021. In 2020, Nigeria took the third place in crypto transactions, after the US and Russia, having performed over USD400 million worth of cryptos. So, it seems that the underline technologies of eNaira are very solid and risk free.

If you go back to the beginning right now and look at all transactions that have ever been done in Bitcoin, you'll see there are literally 100,000 of crypto assets that use the same underlying technology the eNaira is using. There's no fraudster who has ever succeeded in cracking Bitcoins or Ethereum. From this key point, one would want to say that eNaira is very solid and safe.

But there are still challenges confronting the use of eNaira and digital currencies in general. One of the significant risks attributed to the increasing use of digital currency is payment fraud which can be done in various ways. For example, cybercriminals can complete unauthorized or fraudulent transactions.

Phishing

This is a form of cybercrime where cybercriminals steal confidential personal or corporate information. They often use various tactics to collect or trick app users into giving up their login or sign-up details. This is often done through app cloning, deceptive emails, phishing websites, fake text messages or fake phone alerts.

For example, merely two days after the launch of the eNaira, the e-Naira, the Central Bank of Nigeria alerted Nigerians of a fake e-Naira twitter handle (@e-Naira_cbdc) purported to belong to the CBN, that was sending messages relating to the digital currency so as to woo unsuspecting victims. A statement from CBN reads:

"Following the formal launch of the eNaira on Monday, October 25, 2021, the attention of the Central Bank of Nigeria (CBN) has been drawn to criminal and illegal activities of some individuals and a fraudulent twitter handle, @enaira_cbdc purported to belong to the Bank.

"The impostor handle and fraudulent persons have been posting messages related to the eNaira with the intent of wooing unsuspecting Nigerians with claims that the Central Bank of Nigeria (CBN), among other falsities, is disbursing the sum of 50 Billion eNaira currency.

These impostors are bent on defrauding innocent and unsuspecting members of the public through the links attached to their messages for application to obtain eNaira wallets and become beneficiaries of the said 50 billion eNaira currency.

For the avoidance of doubt, the Central of Nigeria (CBN) is not the owner of that twitter handle (@enaira_cbdc) and indeed suspended its presence on Twitter following the Federal Government's Ban."

Other challenges that may confront eNaira are as follows:

- Fraudulent or illegal payments
- Malware or other forms of infection of computers/mobile devices
- Infiltration of company networks
- Internal manipulation (for example within a bank)
- Data theft
- Sanctions or breach of embargos

Since digital money is not transferred physically, it is very difficult to know the person on the other side of a transaction. This makes it easy for cybercriminals to collect sensitive information or scam people through digital currencies like eNaira that is still very much new to many Nigerians.

Nowadays, the complexity of fraud completed by scammers and cybercriminals' is very much on the rise. Cybercrime is on the rise on daily basis, and shows no signs of declining. Modern-day cyber criminals are continuously inventing new crafts for exploiting digital currency users' weaknesses.

They also devise various methods of manipulating digital currencies. They are so much persistent in their efforts to attack payment systems that if they face challenges on one payment method, they can manipulate their ways and shift their focus to other methods.

2. What is the eNaira Speed Wallet?

The eNaira speed wallet is a digital storage for the eNaira. It is held and managed on a distributed ledger. You need to download and install the eNaira Speed Wallet app on your device before you can access, hold or use eNaira.

2.1. Registration Requirements, Transaction Limits & Balances

As drawn out by CBN, there are transaction and wallet balance limits for individual (non-merchant) eNaira wallets. These are the available categories:

Tier 0 - Unbanked customers who have phone numbers and are awaiting **NIN** (National Identity Number) verification: The minimum requirement for this category of people is that they are expected to register with their phone numbers. The daily transaction limit is 20,000 naira, and wallet balance limit is 120,000 naira.

Tier 1 - Customers who have phone numbers, existing bank accounts, and are NIN-verified: The daily transaction limit is 50,000 naira, and wallet balance limit is 300,000 naira.

Tier 2 - Customers who have phone number, existing bank accounts and are NIN-verified: The daily transaction limit is 200,000 naira, and wallet balance limit is 500,000 naira.

Tier 3 - Customers who have existing bank accounts and are NIN-verified: The daily transaction limit is 1,000,000 naira, and wallet balance limit is 5,000,000 naira.

Merchants – No limit on daily transactions and wallet balance.

2.3. Five Types of eNaira Wallets

According to CBN, the eNaira platform hosts 5 different types of eNaira wallets for different stakeholders. They are as follows:

2.3.1. eNaira Stock Wallet

This belongs solely to the CBN that provides a warehouse for all minted eNaira.

2.3.2. eNaira Treasury Wallet

This is maintained by a financial institution (FI). An FI has only one treasury eNaira wallet for warehousing the eNaira it receives from the CBN's eNaira stock wallet. An FI is allowed to create eNaira sub-treasury wallets for its branches, and fund them from the single eNaira treasury wallet it holds with the CBN.

2.3.3. eNaira Branch Wallet

An FI may create eNaira branch wallets (sub-wallets) for its branches. The eNaira branch wallets shall be funded from the FI's treasury eNaira wallet.

2.3.4. eNaira Speed Merchant Wallet

eNaira Merchant speed wallet is to be used by a business mainly for making and receiving eNaira payments for goods and services.

2.3.5. eNaira Speed Wallet

An eNaira speed wallet is available for individuals or end users to transact with on the eNaira platform.

2.4. eNaira Speed Wallet versus eNaira Speed Merchant Wallet

According to CBN, the eNaira Speed Wallet, a fast and easy way for *individual* bank customers to conduct financial transactions. But if you're doing *business*, the eNaira Speed Merchant Wallet is the right app for you. This book will show you step by step how to setup these two types of wallet.

2.5. How to Download & Setup eNaira Speed Wallet

I will use screenshots to show you how to easily download this app. Go to your **Google Play Store** on your Android phone or tablet, and search for *eNaira wallet* or *eNaira Speed wallet* app. If you use an iphone or ipad, download the app from the Apple Store. Alternatively, you can follow this short link to download the app from Play Store: https://bit.ly/3pElvlY.

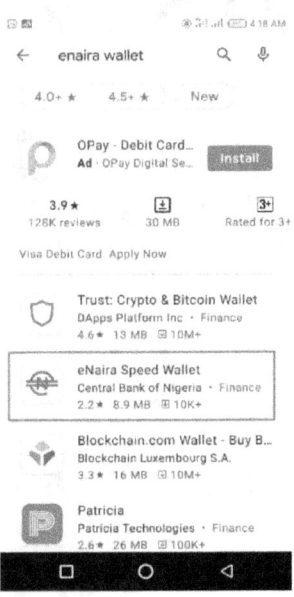

Fig. 2.5.1: How to search for the eNaira Speed Wallet app

To see the app's profile, tap the eNaira icon shown inside the red box in Fig. 2.5.1. Here's how the app's profile page looks like.

Fig. 2.5.2: eNaira Speed Wallet app's profile page on Google Play Store

As you can see the app is light as it's below 10MB in size. However, it has an average rating of 3.0. I think people don't enjoy the app much at the time of writing. Still, I went ahead to begin my installation by taping the **Install** button.

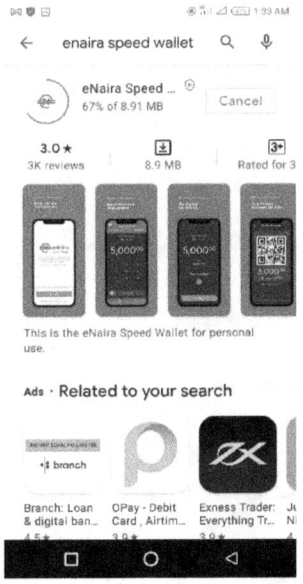

Fig. 2.5.3: eNaira Speed Wallet app is being downloaded from the Play Store

The app should start downloading after a few seconds. See Fig. 2.5.3. In a minute or so, the download should complete. Then search for the app's icon on your Android phone and tap it to launch the app. I had a good first impression, as the app's interface looks rather nice. The first screen that should come up is the login page shown by the screenshot in Fig. 2.5.4.

Fig. 2.5.4: The login screen for the eNaira Speed Wallet

If you don't have login details, maybe because you've installed the app for the first time on your phone, just tap the **Sign up** button at the bottom.

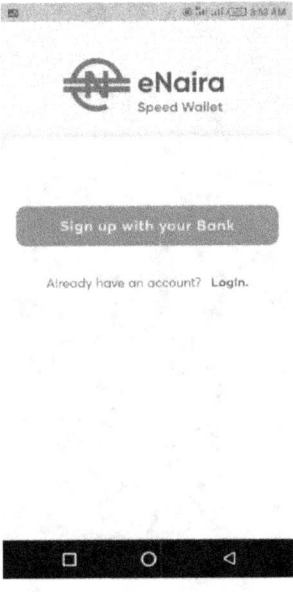

Fig. 2.5.5: The sign up screen

Obviously, you need to have a bank account before you can sign up, so quickly get your bank account details handy. Then tap the **Sign up with your Bank** button. Here's the next screen you should see.

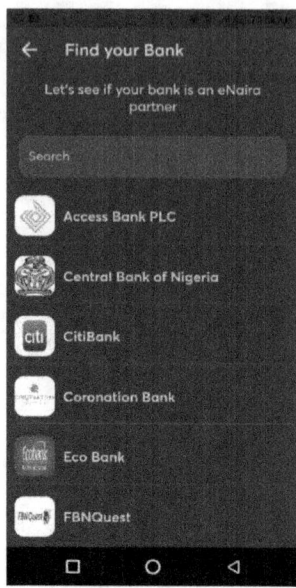

*Fig. 2.5.6: The **Find Your Bank** screen*

You can scroll up or down to find *your* bank's name/logo among a bunch of banks on the screen. Alternatively, you can just use the search box at the top to search your bank. At the time of writing, only 23 banks were added to the eNaira platform. You may find your own bank after scrolling down a little.

Don't feel bad if your bank is not yet added. You can just try again later. I will use Stanbic IBTC Bank as an example in this book. Tap on your bank's logo, and you should be taken to the screen shown in Fig. 2.5.7.

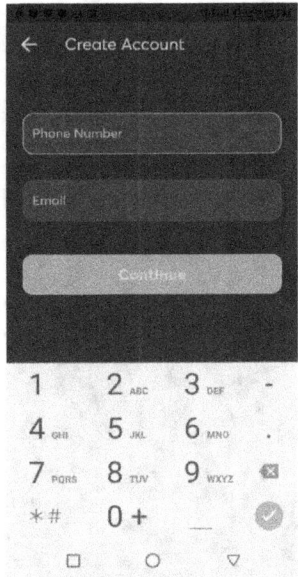

Fig. 2.5.7: The screen for creating an account

To create your account, enter your mobile phone number in the **Phone Number** field at the top. Also enter your email address in the **Email** field. This should activate the *Continue* button. Tap the **Continue** to move on.

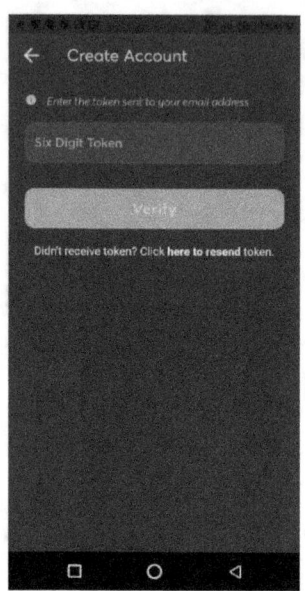

Fig. 2.5.8: The screen for verifying your email address with a 6-digit token

At this point, a **6-digit token** (verification code) should be waiting for your email inbox. If you don't find it there, check your Spam/Junk folder. Your **token expires in 10 minutes**. See Fig. 2.5.9.

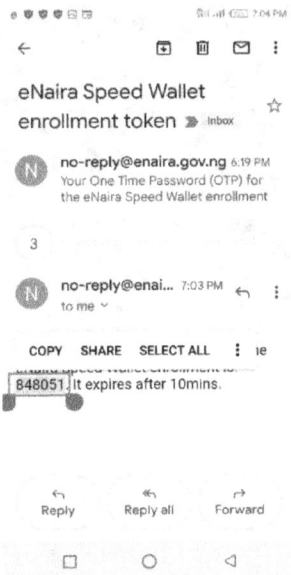

Fig. 2.5.9: How to copy your 6-digit token from your email inbox/spam/junk folder

To copy your token, press and hold your finger on it until it is selected completely as shown. Then tap the **COPY** button. Now, go back to your app and paste your token as shown in Fig. 2.5.10.

Fig. 2.5.10: How to paste your 6-digit token on the app

Tap the **Verify** button to move to the next step.

Fig. 2.5.11: How to enter your password on the app

Also create and enter a password in the **Enter Password** field. A minimum of 12 characters are allowed. You can reveal your password by tapping on the eye icon on the right. To copy your password, press and hold your finger on it.

Re-enter your password again in the **Confirm Password** field, or simply paste it in if you copied it from the previous step. I strongly recommend creating a password with a mixture of numeric, lower-case and upper-case letters. Add at least one special character to your password to make it strong, as illustrated in Fig. 2.5.11. Tap the **Continue** to move on.

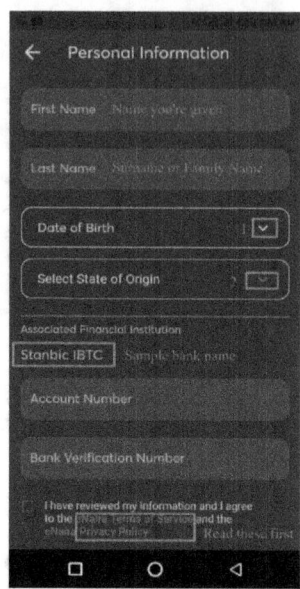

Fig. 2.5.12: How to enter your personal information on the app

Enter your first/given name in the *First Name* field at the top. Also enter your last name (surname or family name) in the *Last Name* field. To enter your *Date of Birth*, tap the down arrow (1) on the right. You should be taken to the screen shown in Fig. 2.5.13.

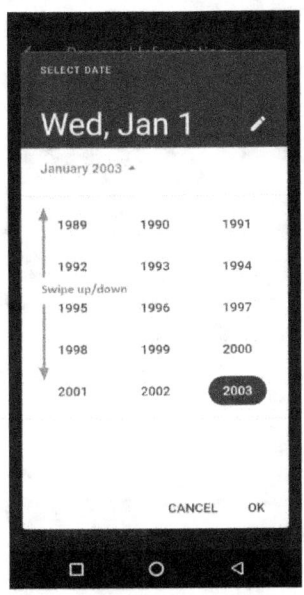

Fig. 2.5.13: How to search your date of birth

Swipe the screen up or down to search for the year. Once you find it, tap it. This should take you to the screen shown in Fig. 2.5.14.

Fig. 2.5.14: How to search your month

Tap the right- or left-pointing arrow at the top to change the calendar month showing on your screen. Once you've found your own month, tap your day on the calendar to complete your date of birth entry. Finally, tap the **OK** button to exit the screen.

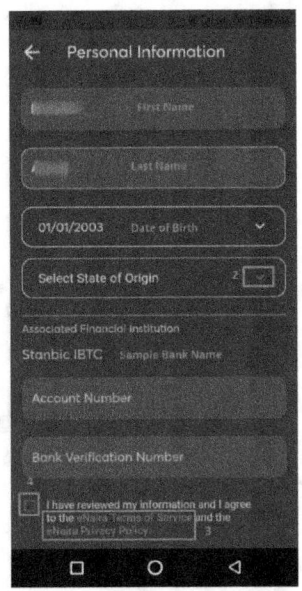

Fig. 2.5.15: Personal information is partly completed on this screen

To select your State of Origin, tap the down arrow (2).

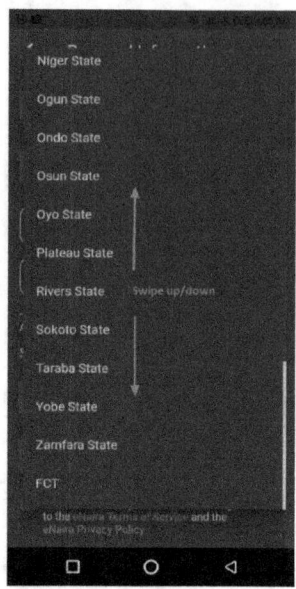

Fig. 2.5.16: How to select your State of Origin

Swipe your screen up or down to search for your State of Origin. Once you find it, tap it to exit the screen shown in Fig. 2.5.17.

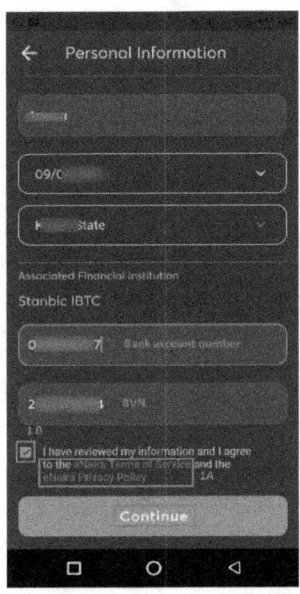

Fig. 2.5.17: How to enter your bank account number and Bank verification Number (BVN)

Enter your bank account number and BVN in the appropriate fields. Tap any of the blue links to go and review the *eNaira Terms of Service* and *Privacy Policy* (1A). Once you're done reviewing, come back to the app and check the small box (1B) to indicate you agree with the terms and policy. Finally, tap the **Continue** button (2) to move on.

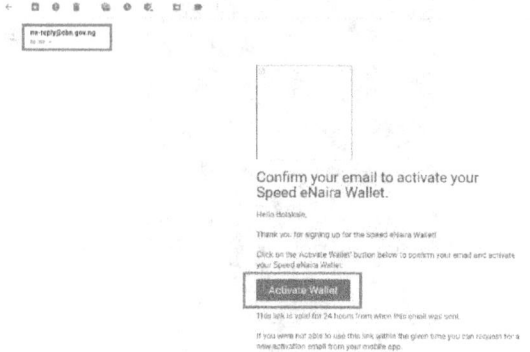

Fig. 2.5.18: Email activation message

On successfully completing your setup, an email will be sent to your inbox from no-reply@cbn.gov.ng you should get a link inside an email sent to your inbox from *no-reply@cbn.gov.ng*, like the shown in Fig. 2.5.18. This link is valid for only 24 hours.

Tap **the Activate Wallet** button to activate your wallet. Don't worry if your registration is unsuccessful. You can go back to retry. Alternatively, you can uninstall the app, reinstall it and then try again. You can also visit your bank to lay your complaints.

Another thing you can do is just call your bank, go to Play Store to read messages from people having similar issues and how they got help, or even compose an email to your bank representative, making sure you include necessary screenshots as proof. You should be able to get help.

The first day I did my registration, it was not successful. I kept getting error messages about my email address not linked to my BVN. So, I called GTB customer service and explained politely that my email address is linked to my BVN. The representative who spoke with me promised to help in at most 48 hours. The second day I tried it again and it worked!

You can now go back to the app and login. You can start using wallet immediately. Here's a shortened link to video (watch from 4:25 min) that shows various features and functionalities of the wallet after logging in: https://bit.ly/319QhjT.

2.6. How to Download & Setup eNaira Speed Merchant Wallet

Again, I will use screenshots to show you how to easily download this Merchant app. Go to your **Google Play Store** on your Android phone or tablet, and search for *eNaira Speed Merchant wallet*. If you use an iphone or ipad, download the app from the Apple Store.

Alternatively, you can follow this short link to download the app from Play Store: https://bit.ly/2XMeGuF. Tap the **Install** button to begin your installation. Here's how the app's download page looks like.

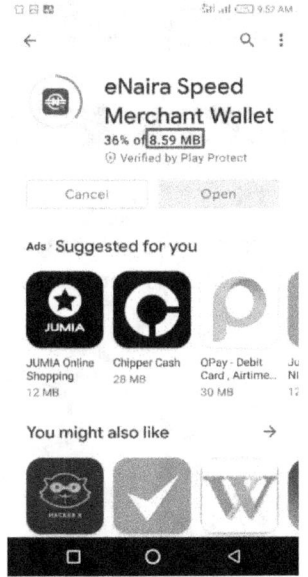

Fig. 2.6.1: eNaira Speed Merchant Wallet app's profile page on Google Play Store

33

You can see from Fig. 2.6.1 that this app too is light because it's below 10MB in size. However, it has an average rating of 2.7 at the time of writing. I think very few people like this app. Still, I went ahead to launch the app by taping the **Open** button.

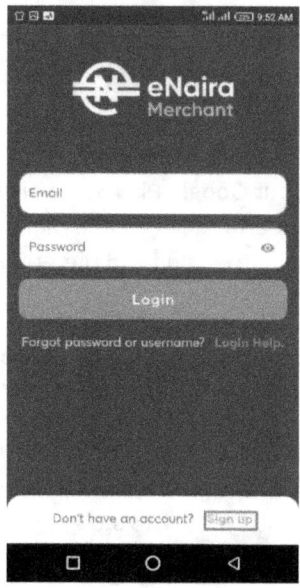

Fig. 2.6.2: The login screen for the eNaira Merchant Wallet

If you don't have login details, maybe because you've installed the app for the first time on your phone, just tap the **Sign up** button at the bottom.

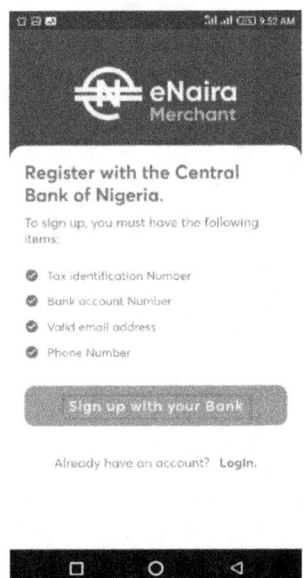

Fig. 2.6.3: The sign up screen for the eNaira Merchant Wallet

Obviously, you need to have a **business bank account** before you can sign up, so quickly get your bank account details handy. You also need the following items:

- TIN (Tax Identification Number)
- Bank account number
- A valid email address
- Business Phone Number

Then tap the **Sign up with your Bank** button. Here's the next screen you should see.

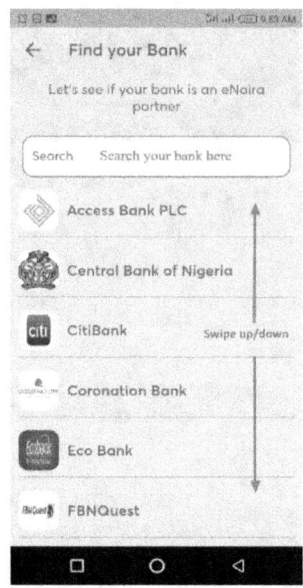

Fig. 2.6.4: How to find your bank

You can scroll up or down to find *your* bank's name/logo among a bunch of banks on the screen. Alternatively, you can just use the search box at the top to search your bank. At the time of writing, only 23 banks were added to the eNaira merchant platform as well.

Don't feel bad if your bank is not yet added. You can just try again later. For me I found my bank, Guaranty Trust Bank (GTB), after scrolling down a little. Tap on your bank's logo, and you should be taken to the screen shown in Fig. 2.6.5.

Fig. 2.6.5: Step 1 of creating an eNaira merchant account

To create your account, enter your **First Name** (your given name), **Last Name** (surname or family name), the **BVN** (Bank Verification Number) of the main signatory to your business account, **Email** address, and **Phone Number** in their respective fields as shown in Fig. 2.6.5.

To select your **State of Origin**, tap the down arrow. Swipe your screen up or down to search for your State. Once you find it, tap it. You will be taken back to the previous screen. Repeat the process to enter your **Date of Birth**. Once you find it, tap it to exit the screen and move to the screen shown in Fig. 2.6.6.

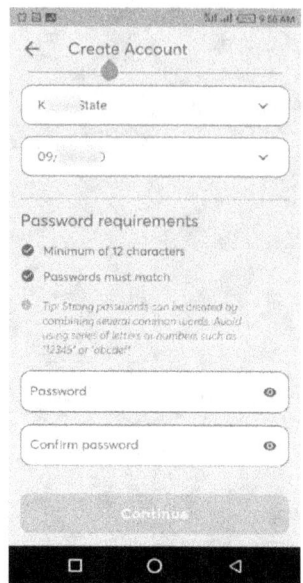

Fig. 2.6.6: Step 2 of creating an eNaira merchant account

Also create and enter a password in the third field. A minimum of 12 characters are allowed. I strongly recommend creating a password with a mixture of numeric, lower-case and upper-case letters. Add at least one special character to your password to make it very strong.

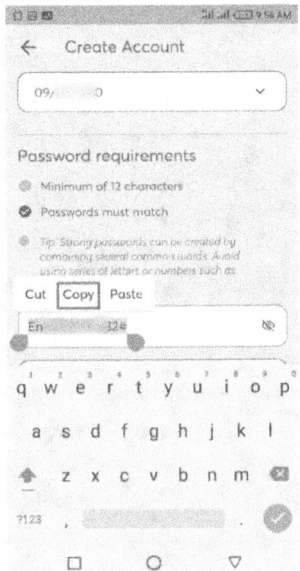

Fig. 2.6.7: Step 3 of creating an eNaira merchant account - How to copy your password

You can reveal your password by tapping on the eye icon on the right. To copy your password, press and hold your finger on it.

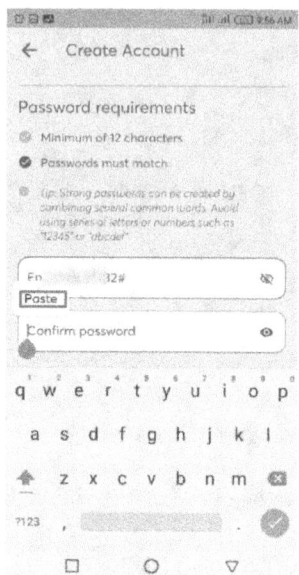

Fig. 2.6.8: Step 4 of creating an eNaira merchant account - How to paste your password in the Confirm password field

Then paste your password, or simply re-enter it, in the *Confirm password* field to confirm it. At this point, the **Continue** button should be active.

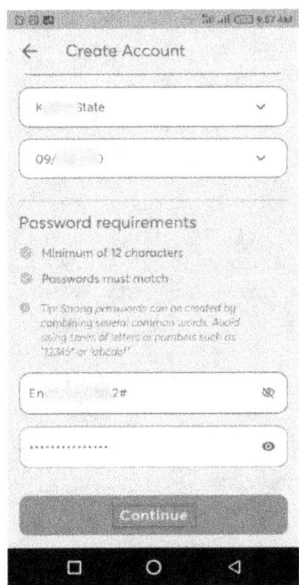

*Fig. 2.6.9: Step 5 of creating an eNaira merchant account – Click the **Continue** button*

Finally, tap it to move on.

Fig. 2.6.10: Step 6 of creating an eNaira merchant account – Fill in your business information

Now fill in your **Legal Business Name** and **Trading Business Name**. First, you must know that there's an important difference between a legal name and a trade name. The legal name is the name of a person or the entity that owns the business. The legal name must be registered with CAC (Corporate Affairs Commission) in Nigeria, and it generally has a legal ending like LTD, LLP or LLC, after the title. A legal name is used in all communications with the government.

On the other hand, a trade name is, in general, the name your business uses for sales and advertising purposes. Sometimes you can refer to a trade name as "doing business as (DBA)" or a "fictitious" title. Here's a good example. "McDonald's" is the trade name of a business, but the legal name of the business is "McDonald's Corporation."

Now add your **RC Number** (company's registration number). Then tap the down arrow on the right side of **Select Business Category** field shown in Fig. 2.6.10.

Fig. 2.6.11: Step 7A of creating an eNaira merchant account – select your business category

Swap this screen up or down to search for the category of your business. If the right category is not included, select **Other** as shown in Fig. 2.6.11.

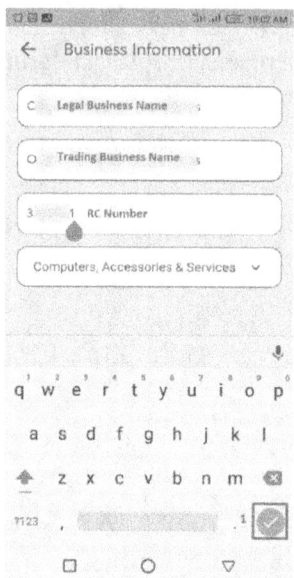

Fig. 2.6.12: Step 7B of creating an eNaira merchant account – Business category is selected

Tap the check mark (1) at the bottom of the screen to move to the next step.

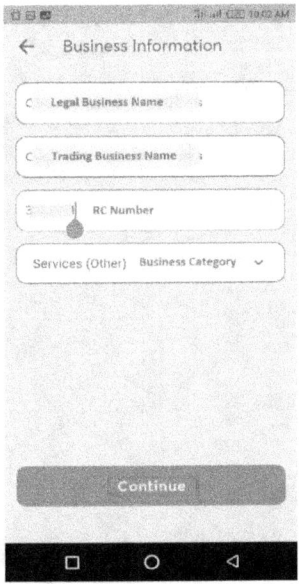

Fig. 2.6.13: Creating an eNaira merchant account is completed

Tap the **Continue** button at the bottom of the screen to move to the Review screen.

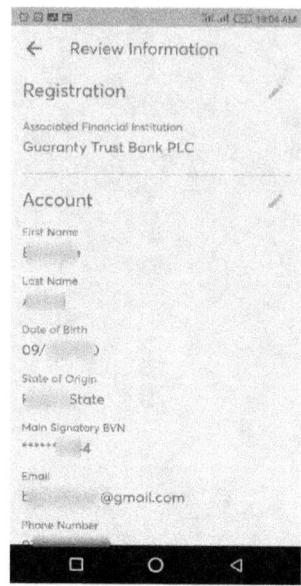

Fig. 2.6.14: First screen of the business registration review

Swipe the screen to review more of your business information. See Fig. 2.6.15.

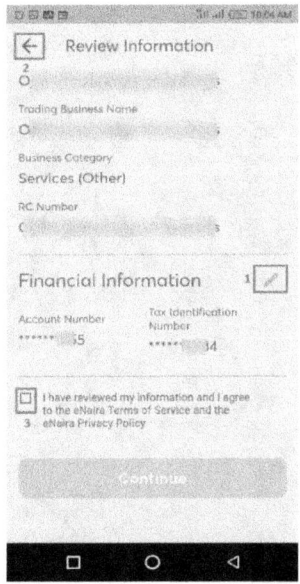

Fig. 2.6.15: Second screen of the business registration review

If you want to make some changes, tap the pencil icon (1) to make edits, or tap the back arrow (2) at the top to go back. Otherwise, tap any of the blue links to go and review the *eNaira Terms of Service and Privacy Policy*. Once you're done reviewing, come back to the app and check the small box (3) to indicate you agree with the terms and policy.

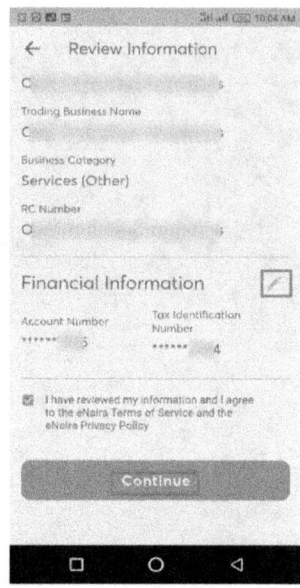

Fig. 2.6.16: Second screen of the business registration review with the Continue button activated

Finally, tap the **Continue** button (2) to move on.

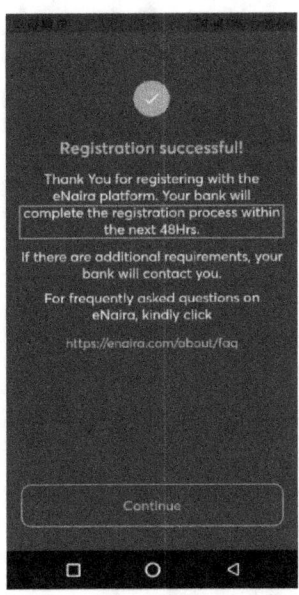

Fig. 2.6.17: Confirmation of successful registration of the eNaira Speed Merchant Wallet

As you can see in Fig. 2.6.17, my bank should complete the registration process within the next 48 hours. I the meantime, you can check out your wallet! Click the Continue button to move on to the login screen. See Fig. 2.6.18.

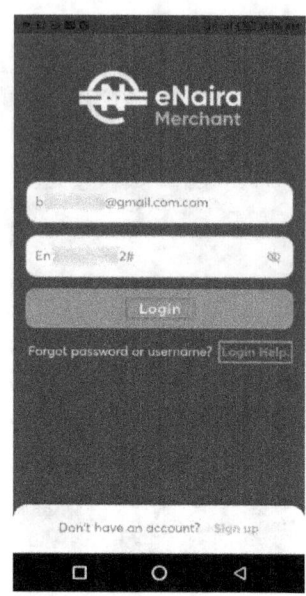

Fig. 2.6.18: The login screen for the eNaira Speed Merchant Wallet

To login to your merchant wallet, you have to first enter your **username** and **password**. Your username is the email address you submitted at the time of registration. Then tap the **Login** button. If you forgot your password, or if you need help with logging, tap the **Login Help** button.

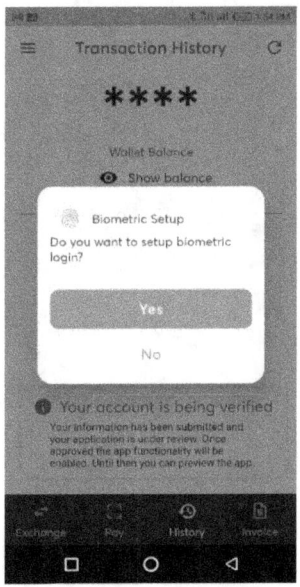

Fig. 2.6.19: The wallet transaction history page (behind) showing a pop-up window (in the front) asking if I want to setup a biometric login

Boom! Here comes the transaction history page (see Fig. 2.6.19) showing my **account is being verified**. There's also a small window that pops up asking if you want to setup a **biometric login**. If you want to, tap the **Yes** button, otherwise tap **No** to close the pop-up window.

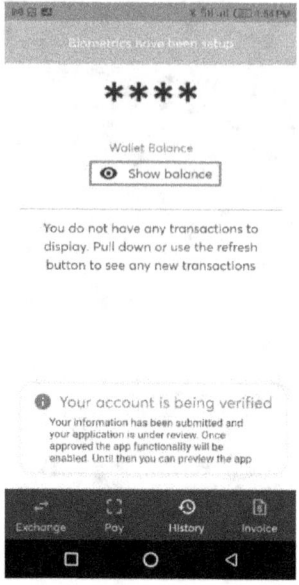

Fig. 2.6.20: The wallet history page showing an eye icon for checking my balance and a notification banner at the top that confirms my biometric logging is set up.

You can tap the eye icon (**Show balance**) to view your wallet balance, but don't be disappointed to see 0.00 eNaira. This is because your bank has some work to do on your wallet. See Fig. 2.6.21.

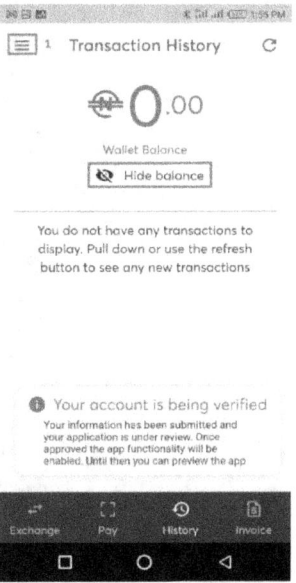

Fig. 2.6.21: The wallet history page showing my wallet is currently empty

In the mean time, tap the menu icon (1) to check out more features or functionalities of the app.

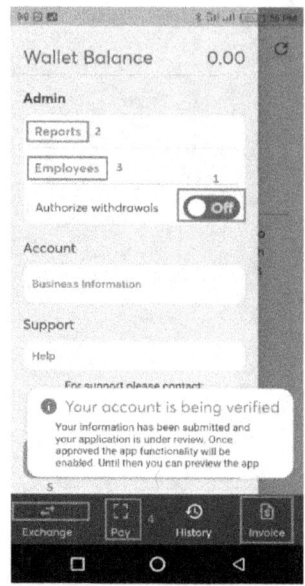

Fig. 2.6.22: The Admin section of the app showing

For example, in the **Admin** section shown in Fig. 2.6.22, you can toggle the **On/Off** button (1) to **authorize or unauthorize withdrawals**. You also have links to Transaction **Reports** (2). You can create permissions for **Employees** (3) and/or enable/disable their accounts. Tap the **Pay** button (4) at the bottom to see more features of the app.

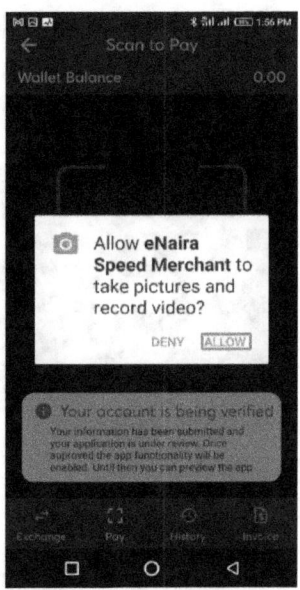

Fig. 2.6.23: App is asking for permissions to access certain phone functions

Tap the **Allow** button to give your app the necessary permissions it needs.

Fig. 2.6.24: The phone camera is enabled to scan a QR code for payment

Giving the eNaira app permissions allow it to automatically activate the phone camera for scanning a QR code for making payments.

Tap the **Exchange** button (5) at the bottom of Fig. 2.6.22 to see more another exciting feature of the app.

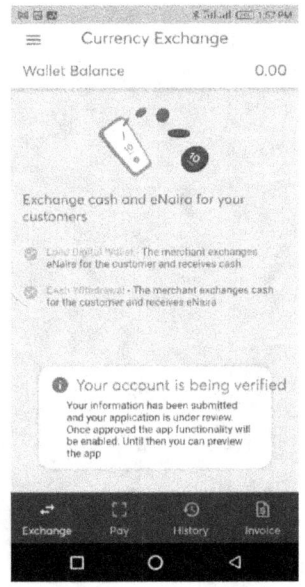

Fig. 2.6.25: The Currency Exchange section of the App

In this section you can exchange Naira to eNaira or eNaira to Naira for your customers. Now tap the **Invoice** button (6) in Fig. 2.6.22.

Fig. 2.6.26: The Invoice section of the App

From Fig. 2.6.26, you can see that you can also generate invoices with the eNaira merchant app. Now, I want you to check out the **log out** function of the app. You have to back to the Admin section to see the log out button. See Fig. 2.6.27.

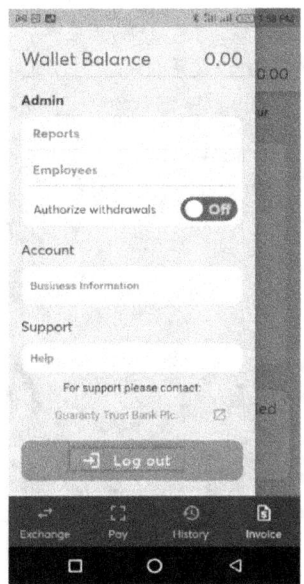

Fig. 2.6.27: The Log out button of the App

When you tap the log out button, the screen shown in Fig. 2.6.28 comes up.

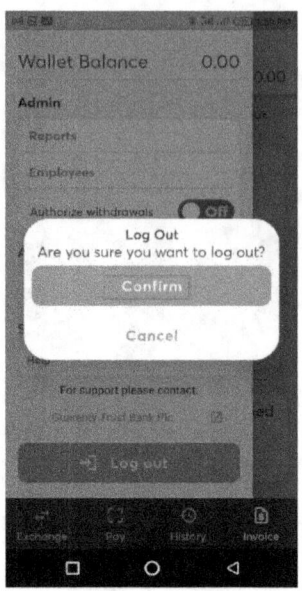

Fig. 2.6.28: The Log out confirmation

Tap **Confirm** to confirm you really want to log out.

Fig. 2.6.29: I'm logged out successfully

Click **Done** to exit the screen shown in Fig. 2.6.29 and return to the login screen shown in Fig. 2.6.30.

Fig. 2.6.30: The login screen now has a biometric icon for logging in with my finger prints

Now that you're back at the login screen, the first thing you notice is that you can log in with a finger print. Try doing this right now. For me I was surprised it did not work! When I touched my phone's fingerprint scanner to login to the app, nothing happened. Seriously! So, I had to login to the app with only my username and password. Obviously, this app needs update!

3. The Good, The Bad & The Ugly

In this chapter, I'll tell you what I think is good, what is bad and what is ugly about the two eNaira wallets I have tested so far.

3.1 My Evaluation

As you must have seen, this book it titled "eNaira Speed Wallet: The good, The Bad and The Ugly". So, now I will give you my take on what comes under each of these headings. But first, let's see how I evaluated the app.

The first time I installed the **eNaira Speed Wallet** app on my Android phone, it did not work. I completed all the steps of the registration but the app failed to register me. In addition, I could not even login to the app with the login details I created successfully. However, I was successful with the app on the second day, and that's after CBN updated the app.

After installing the **eNaira Speed Merchant Wallet** app on the same Android phone, I completed all the steps of the registration (see Chapter 2.6) the app registered my business bank account successfully. In addition, I could login to the app with the login details I created and check out a bunch of other features of the app.

3.3.1 The Good Sides of eNaira Wallets

1. First, I have to admit that the interfaces of both wallets look rather nice, to my eyes at least, and it's easy to create accounts with them.

2. Navigation is easy on both apps, and should not confuse a first-time user of the apps.

3. The apps are very light-weight because both are less than 10MB, which is the standard for the mobile app industry.

4. The apps respond very fast when in use. No hanging or sluggishness of any sort.

5. The icons used for the apps are noticeably different so it's easy for users to identify without getting confused. The fact that both apps can be installed on the same phone despite the fact that they are a little similar.

6. I like the additional security feature (biometric) embedded in the eNaira Speed Merchant Wallet. This is very good for businesses and corporate organizations.

3.3.2 The Bad Sides of eNaira Wallets

1. The first release of the eNaira Speed Wallet app was a disgrace to the Central Bank of Nigeria. I'm highly disappointed that after taking pains to supply my registration details, the wallet simply did not work. This is very bad. It didn't do a thing. Even after reinstalling the first release of the app several times, it continued to give meaningless error messages like the following:

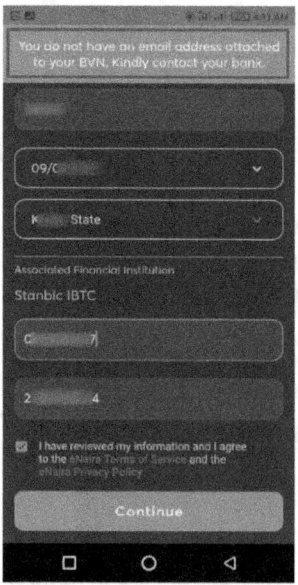

Fig. 3.1.1: Incorrect error message about email addresses not linked to BVN

I registered my email and BVN with my bank, so I did not deserve this kind of error.

2. That day I went out to the Play Store to check out what Nigerians are saying about the tap, and I became even more disappointed. It seems that CBN were only in hurry to roll out the app but cared less about the functionality of the app. The following screenshots show more of my findings on Play Store.

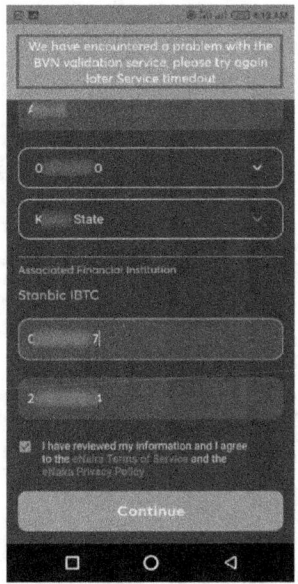

Fig. 3.1.2: App encountered a problem with BVN validation service

Fig. 3.1.2 is another error that many of the first-time app users receive. I studied many of the reviews on the Play Store and I was very appalled at the tons of complaints I saw.

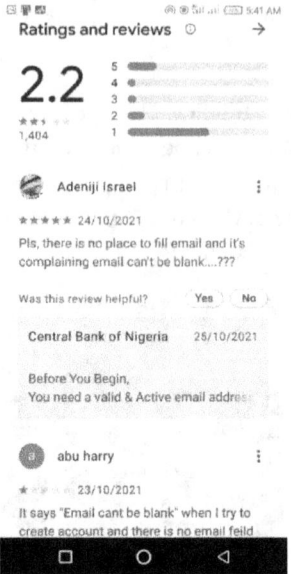

Fig. 3.1.3: App encountered "Email can't be blank" problem

There was no field to fill in email address on the first release of the app but the app complained "Email can't be blank".

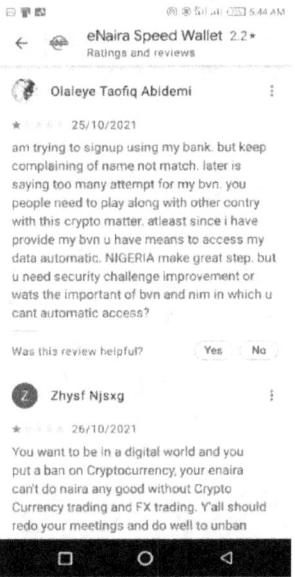

Fig. 3.1.4: App encountered "Names do not match" problem

Another notorious error message the first release of the app generated is names mismatch errors when there were nothing of such.

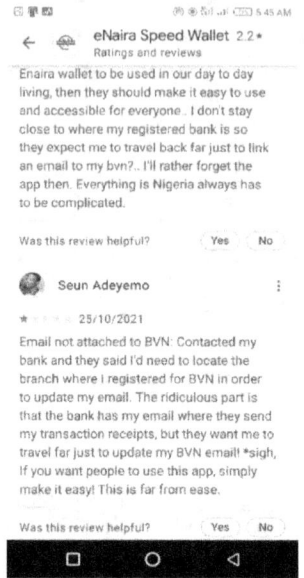

Fig. 3.1.5: App users unable to get help from their banks

Even more disheartening was the fact that some app users were unable to get help from their banks concerning the issue of emails and BVNs.

3.3.3 The Ugly Sides of eNaira Wallets

1. I spoke to many people on social media concerning their success with the app but again, the response I got is embarrassingly overwhelming. It seems that an overwhelming majority of people, home and abroad, have still not been able to register accounts on either the first or second release app.

2. The number of digital currencies allocated to the wallets is ridiculously too small. The 500-million eNaira that CBN said they have minted is far too small to encourage Nigerians (home or abroad) to use the wallets. This constraint should be removed.

3. The number of banks participating in the project is too small. This is another constraint that should be removed.

4. Sadly, I discovered that while CBN had removed the first version/release of the eNaira Speed wallet app was later in the day from the Play Store, they made it very much available with its tons of issues on the Apple Store. This confused both Android and iOS users.

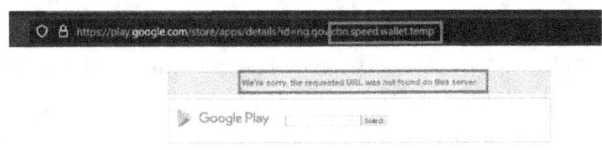

Fig. 3.1.6: App vanished from Google Play Store!

5. The second day, an updated version (the second release) of the eNaira Speed Wallet was hurriedly launched on Google Store with a slight change made to its name. It is now called *eNaira Speed Wallet (Individual)*!

6. Even with the release of the "updated" version, users are neither allowed to change their accounts within the same bank, nor re-register the app with a different bank. Why put this constraint CBN? I know CBN is well aware that many Nigerians have more than one bank accounts!

7. Verification of accounts take more that the 48 hours that the banks promised. Banks need to work faster.

3.3.4. People Experiencing Trouble with the eNaira Wallets & Why CBN is Unable to Find a Fix

I think that CBN removed the first version eNaira Speed Wallet app (the merchant one is still available) after receiving a ton of complaints from Nigerians who have tried creating accounts on the app but unsuccessful. I noticed that many people and businesses, including financial institutions, who have given the both versions a try are not happy with apps and the restrictions placed within the wallets.

If CBN refuses to slow down and make greater effort to improve the eNaira project, they will neither be unable to find a lasting solution to the problem, nor create good and safe wallets.

The kind of attitude CBN is demonstrating is not only detrimental to the overall image of the apex bank in Nigeria, but it's also an ugly disgrace on Nigeria at large! This will have a negative effect on both the Naira and eNaira.

3.2. Conclusion

I think the rollout of the eNaira wallets should be relatively slow. More time, effort and resources need to be allocated to this project. I strongly advise CBN to outsource the project to the experts in the field of cryptocurrency.

Even if it'll take quite a long time before lots and lots of people start using it, it will be successful in the end. For now, I can only hope that CBN and all the parties concerned can learn their lesson that this kind of project is not supposed to be rushed.

But what do *you* think about the eNaira wallets? Please send me an email to let me know what you think. I'll get back to you quickly. At Ojula Technology Innovations, we hope to put more of books like this out again very soon.

Cheers,

Ojula Technology Innovations

Bolakalearemu2021@gmail.com

www.ingramcontent.com/pod-product-compliance
Lightning Source LLC
Chambersburg PA
CBHW071147240526
45465CB00024BA/1857